Good Day Bad Day

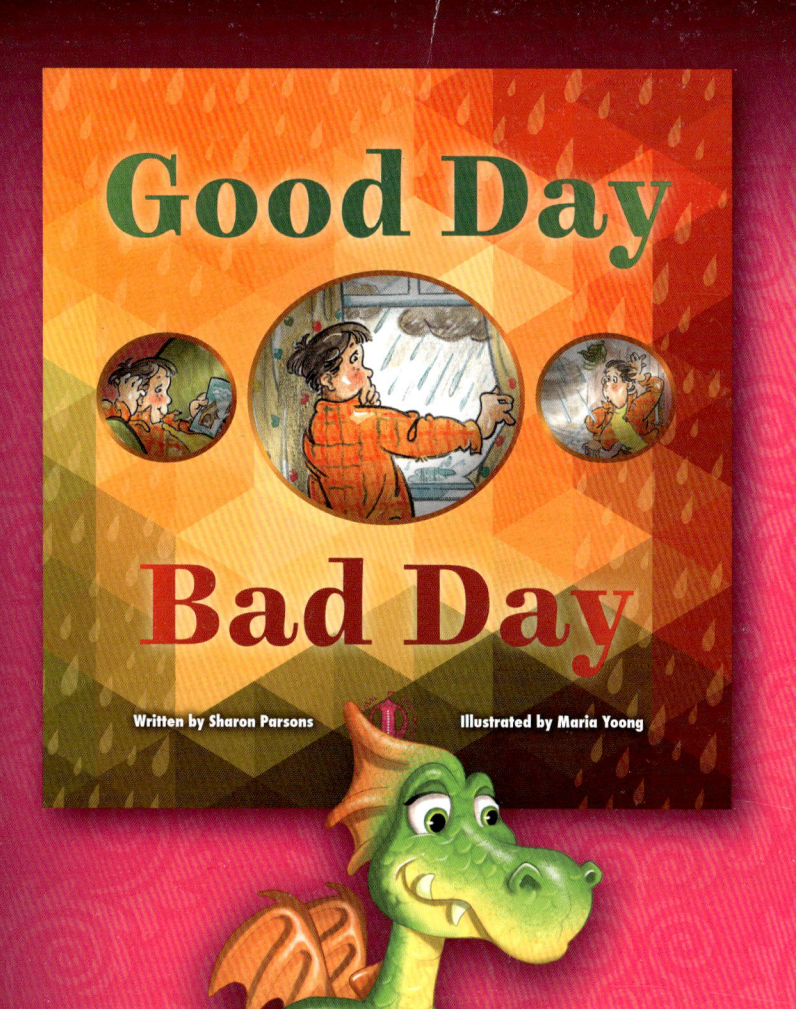

Written by Sharon Parsons
Illustrated by Maria Yoong

a boy

a bad day

"This book is about a boy who finds a good way to spend a bad day. I hope you have a good day too!"

Grusilda xxx

Is it a good day to play with the ball?

No, it is a bad day to play with the ball.

Is it a good day to go to the beach?

No, it is a bad day to go to the beach.

Is it a good day to read a book?

Yes, it is a good day to read a book.

Every day is a good day to read a book.